My Life with
Deafness

written by **Mari Schuh** • art by **Isabel Muñoz**

AMICUS ILLUSTRATED and AMICUS INK
are published by Amicus
P.O. Box 227, Mankato, MN 56002
www.amicuspublishing.us

Editor: Gillia Olson
Designer: Kathleen Petelinsek

Library of Congress Cataloging-in-Publication Data
Names: Schuh, Mari C., 1975- author. | Muñoz, Isabel, illustrator.
Title: My life with deafness / Mari Schuh ; illustrated by Isabel Muñoz.
Description: Mankato, Minnesota : Amicus, [2021] | Series: My life with... | Includes bibliographical references. | Audience: Ages 6-9 |
Audience: Grades 2-3 | Summary: "Meet Danton! He loves his dogs and playing football. He's also deaf. Danton is real and so are his
experiences. Learn about his life in this illustrated narrative nonfiction picture book for elementary students"– Provided by publisher.
Identifiers: LCCN 2019047375 (print) | LCCN 2019047376 (ebook) | ISBN 9781681519906 (library
binding) | ISBN 9781681526379 (paperback) | ISBN 9781645490753 (pdf)
Subjects: LCSH: Deaf children–United States–Biography–Juvenile literature. | Deafness in children–Juvenile literature.
Classification: LCC HV2392 .S35 2021 (print) | LCC HV2392 (ebook) | DDC 362.4/2092 [B]–dc23
LC record available at https://lccn.loc.gov/2019047375
LC ebook record available at https://lccn.loc.gov/2019047376

For Danton and his classmates–MS

Thank you to the staff at the Minnesota State Academy
for the Deaf for their assistance with this book.

About the Author

Mari Schuh's love of reading began with cereal boxes at
the kitchen table. Today, she is the author of hundreds of
nonfiction books for beginning readers. With each book, Mari
hopes she's helping kids learn a little bit more about the world
around them. Find out more about her at marischuh.com.

About the Illustrator

To paint for a living was Isabel Muñoz' dream, and now she's
proud to be the illustrator of several children books. Isabel
works from a studio based in a tiny, cloudy, green and lovely
town in the north of Spain. You can follow her at isabelmg.com.

Hey there! My name is Danton. Like a lot of kids, I love to play with my pets. I have two dogs named Lucky and Star. I'm also deaf. I have a fun, busy life. Let me tell you a little about it.

Being deaf means I cannot hear. Instead, I use my other senses. See the words on the bottom of the TV screen? The words are called closed captioning. I read the words when I watch TV. That way, I know what the people on TV are saying.

Babies can be born deaf, like I was. Most babies who are born deaf have parents who can hear. My parents are deaf. My sister is deaf, too.

People can lose their hearing in other ways. A bad head injury can cause hearing loss. Very bad fevers or infections can, too. As adults get older, they might lose their hearing.

Very few people who are deaf have no hearing at all. I can hear some loud sounds. I can hear drums, loud video games, and the car radio when I turn the volume way up.

Some kids at my school wear hearing aids. Hearing aids help people hear sounds they can't hear on their own.

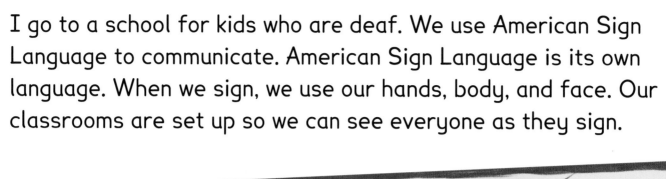

I go to a school for kids who are deaf. We use American Sign Language to communicate. American Sign Language is its own language. When we sign, we use our hands, body, and face. Our classrooms are set up so we can see everyone as they sign.

12

Most people I meet are really nice. But not everyone. One day, a group of kids made fun of me and my friends. They pretended to sign. But they weren't using real sign language. I chose to ignore them.

My school has the same classes as other schools. There are lots of activities, too. We had a reading fair last month. Students read books and then told visitors what we learned.

The spelling bee was held this week. I won first place! We're also getting ready for the school play. This year's play is Rudolph the Red-Nosed Reindeer. I'm playing Rudolph.

After school, I often jump on my trampoline. I'm working on a perfect front flip. Sometimes Mom waves to gets my attention. Then she signs to me. It's time to go inside.

16

Lights flash at my house when
someone rings the doorbell.
I bet my friends are here.

My friends and I play football. I love to run with the ball. I can't always hear people cheer for me. But I can always see them. Touchdown!

Meet Danton

Hi. I am Danton. I live with my mom, dad, and sister, who are also deaf. I go to school at the Minnesota State Academy for the Deaf in Faribault. I love to play sports, have fun outside, and play on my computer. I can be a picky eater. I love chicken but not beef.

Respecting People Who Are Deaf

Treat a person who is deaf like you would any person. Be kind and respectful.

When you communicate, look right at the person. Do not look away or at the sign language interpreter. (Sign language interpreters speak words out loud to explain the meaning of sign language.)

Don't expect the person to be able to read your lips. Reading lips is not always a good way to communicate.

Be mindful of faces you make. The person might worry that you are mad at them, even though you aren't.

It can be hard for a person who is deaf to communicate in the dark. Be mindful during movies and sleepovers.

Do not make up sign language. Ask for help or write a note.

Do not shout. It will not help the person hear you.

To get their attention, gently tap them on the shoulder. Do not suddenly come up behind a person who is deaf and startle them.

Helpful Terms

American Sign Language
A language that uses hand signs, body movements, and emotions shown on the face instead of speech; different hand signs stand for words, letters, and numbers. Different kinds of sign languages are used in different countries and areas around the world.

ASL Alphabet

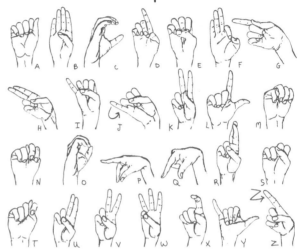

closed captioning Spoken words and other sounds on a TV show or movie that appear on the screen as printed words.

communicate To share thoughts, feelings, ideas, or information with another person.

hearing aid A small piece of electronic equipment that people wear in or behind one or both ears; hearing aids make sounds louder so people can hear them.

Read More

Beese, Lilli. **Proud to Be Deaf**. London: Wayland, 2019.

Chang, Kirsten. **My Friend is Deaf**. All Kinds of Friends. Minneapolis: Bullfrog Books, Jump!, 2020.

Schaefer, Lola M. **Some Kids Are Deaf: a 4D Book**. Understanding Differences. North Mankato, Minn.: Capstone Press, 2018.

Websites

FINGER SPELLING: THE ALPHABET

http://grownups.pbskids.org/arthur/print/signdesign/finger-spelling.html

Learn to sign the letters of the alphabet and numbers 1 to 10.

HEARING LOSS

https://www.cdc.gov/ncbddd/kids/hearing.html

Find helpful information about hearing loss.

PBS: SCIENCE TREK | SOUND: WITHOUT SOUND

https://tpt.pbslearningmedia.org/resource/sound-without-sound-science-trek/

Find out what "sound" means to someone who is deaf.